CRAP MANAGERS
and how to survive them

CRAP MANAGERS
and how to survive them

Margot Lawrence

Margot Lawrence was born in Zimbabwe. She has worked mainly in the charity and public sectors, where her experience of managers has provided an abundance of material for this book. She has written two books on community development, as well as articles for the Guardian, Independent and Daily Telegraph. Margot lives in south London with her family and an old, somewhat stinky basset hound.

CONTENTS

INTRODUCTION

In the silent, still-black dead of night across Britain, people are in bed awake, staring miserably into the darkness, or folded in sleep and having nightmares. The teachers, the civil servants, the social workers, the hospital staff, the receptionists, the journalists, the sales assistants, the charity workers, all tossing and turning in their troubled, fretful sleep. There is probably somebody in your neighbourhood – you'll recognise them by their shadowy, haunted expression. At train stations each weekday you will see herds of these poor shuffling wrecks, victims of a condition known as Crap Manager Syndrome or CMS.

You might well be a sufferer of CMS. Do you wake at three in the morning worrying about something your manager has said to you? Are you anxious and stressed? Do you suffer from low self-esteem and feel that everything you do at work is pointless? Are you frustrated, demotivated, demoralized? Do you fantasise daily about winning the lottery and telling your manager to go and fuck him/herself ?

The problem with crap managers as opposed to difficult colleagues is that they have power over us and can make our working lives hell. The obvious solution if you don't like your manager is to resign, but in the current recession jobs are not readily available, and nobody wants to exchange the one they have for the soul-destroying experience of applying for Jobseeker's Allowance.

What makes a manager crap? Does the job itself have a corrupting effect or is a certain type of person attracted to it? Studies in recent years have shown that a significant number of managers and CEOs have psychopathic tendencies. Known as 'successful psychopaths', the main difference in their behavior to that of rampantly disturbed criminals is that they are generally law-abiding and less impulsive. You may recognize some of their personality traits in your own manager including histrionic behavior, superficial charm, insincerity, egocentricity and the ability to manipulate others for their own ends. Not to mention narcissism, lack of empathy, machiavellianism, perfectionism, workaholism, inflexibility and dictatorial behavior. Sound familiar? Now you know why you don't sleep at night! The very last person you would want to be in control of your life is actually responsible for a large part of your waking hours.

The current culture of top-heavy, absurdly bureaucratic management has invaded all areas of professional life. It was previously associated with the corporate sector, but over the last twenty years, a pestilential plague of managers has been unleashed on the public and charity sectors, who now follow a corporate model. There are managers to manage the managers who manage the managers. It is especially detrimental to small charities who are advised by some funders and management consultants to adopt this model when they simply don't have the resources to sustain it, so they go under, losing vital frontline services.

All the manager types in this book are based on real-life experiences in charities, private companies and government departments. They are mostly drawn from that fertile ground for crap management, the public sector, but crap managers exhibit similar characteristics wherever they work. Bullshitters are bullshitters whether you have to endure their bullshit in a bank or a school. No one escapes crap management, even staff working in life and death situations like the National Health Service, where there are more managers than doctors and nurses. This is supposedly for the benefit of patients, but most people arriving at A&E with a suspected heart attack would rather be greeted by someone in a white coat and stethoscope than a power suit and clipboard.

When you lie awake in the small hours wondering how you will survive another day at work, take comfort in the knowledge that you are not alone. If your manager is jerking you around, go into the toilet and read about Brian the Bully or Nigel the Narcissist and know that we are all in this together!

SECTION 1
The Bullies

Ambitious Manager

When Allyson is asked in a job interview where she sees herself in five years time, she doesn't reply that she hopes she won't be dead or have a horrible disease involving worms – she outlines a formidable strategy of self-advancement.

If Allyson were to depict her career trajectory on a graph, it would show a forty-five degree diagonal from the bottom left-hand corner moving to the top right-hand corner in a seamless line. There is nothing wrong with healthy ambition – it is necessary to succeed in most professions. But Allyson is driven by a self-serving, ruthless streak and doesn't give a shit about her job in your office. She sees it as one small step in her glorious ascent to the top.

You may have been working there for some time, but your sense of timeless consistency will be rudely pierced by the spiked heels of Allyson's power stilettos. Allyson will regard it as a failure if one policy or procedure is left untouched. She has vision, which will be brought to fruition by a hatchet job on the staff team. Allyson regards staff she has to jettison as 'dead wood' and you know what happens to dead wood.

'I hope you don't take this as a criticism.'

You'll find yourself desperately trying not to fall into this category, nodding enthusiastically in meetings and laughing uproariously at Allyson's jokes. You'll hate yourself but bills have to be paid.

Her motto 'No one is indispensible' means that she will slash jobs without a second thought. She won't care if an employee is a single parent with three children, including a daughter who needs dialysis three times a week. Allyson would never let soppy sentiment get in the way of her relentlessly upward career path. She once ran a mail order business and employed her mother for a bit of cheap labour, then sacked her because she thought her old mum's fingers weren't nimble enough on the keyboard. Allyson will only let you go to your grandmother's funeral if it's a quiet day in the office and you've done all your spreadsheets.

Allyson's strategy for dumping staff members who hamper her vision is to force them to re-apply for jobs they've been doing perfectly well. Then she can remove them after she's compelled to make the 'difficult decision' of taking an external candidate who performs better at the interview. If you survive Allyson's streamlining, she'll pack you off to attend a 'Managing Change' workshop to prevent you from having a negative reaction to what she calls 'refocusing the company's skills set'.

Once she has managed to wreck most of the good things in your organisation, Allyson will exit in a blaze of glory for her next job, leaving nothing but half measures and unrealistic working proposals. You will have to repair the damage done by Allyson while she was tinkering.

 **TOP TIP**

FOR DEALING WITH ALLYSON

Grit your teeth and wait. Allyson's career plan dictates that she only stays in a job for three years, so she won't be around for long bcfore she moves on to ruin another organization.

In the meantime, to deflect her from thoughts of your redundancy, bring out the old sycophancy and say: "That 'Managing Change' workshop you sent me to was really inspirational." Inwardly, you can have an imaginary conversation with her, where you deliver a searing invective on her failings while you stamp hard on her stiletto-clad foot.

Micro-Manager

Mags may have a comfy, reassuring name but don't be fooled by this. Mags is a hyper-vigilant, nit-picking micro-manager with an obsessive-compulsive need to control her environment. Mags always looks immaculate, her bleached hair cemented into place. Her home is oppressively tidy with copious, noxious air fresheners everywhere; she believes they are more hygienic than real air is.

Mags views everything as clutter. She will ask you to tidy your desk when all you can see is a hole-punch and two ball-point pens. What Mags would really like to do is sweep away the staff because she secretly feels the office would be much tidier if there were no people in it. She keeps a large vat of disinfectant wipes in the stationery cupboard for everyone to sanitise their phones and desks. She will often spend two or three hours cleaning the surfaces around her work space, wearing a pair of gigantic, extra-thick, plastic gloves to ward off imaginary germs.

In Mags's universe, the slightest mistake heralds catastrophe. Details you might think are of no consequence like putting a stamp upside down on an envelope, will send her into a jittery flurry. The only way she can ward off her visceral fear of losing control is to dominate the staff, and she wears her micro-managing like a badge of honour. As far as she is concerned, hounding staff achieves results. If you are a capable and self-motivated person, it will be unbearable, as Mags will deny you any autonomy or interesting work. She will de-skill you by making you appear to be far less competent than you are. She will monitor your phone calls, edit your emails and scrutinize your written work. She won't let you to make a single work-related decision without her approval. You won't even be allowed to fart without permission! Every time you turn around you'll be aware of the hot breath of Mags down your neck.

Far from being motivated and wanting to give your best, this will make you oppressed and suicidal. You might be tempted to frequent the toilets to escape the misery of the office, but be careful, because your loo visits will be monitored. If you sit in the toilet cubicle so long you have thumbprints on the side of your head from resting it in your hands, Mags's suspicions will be aroused. Just rub your stomach and shrug apologetically to indicate a dicky gut. She might hate or fear you for having diarrhoea but she can't sack you.

Mags embodies crap management with her pathological need for control and she will waste time carrying out unnecessary and inappropriate disciplinary actions on staff members for spurious, microscopic infringements. Don't discuss your toothache with a colleague during office hours within earshot of Mags – she'll slap a verbal warning on you before you can say novocaine.

TOP TIP

FOR DEALING WITH MAGS

When her OCD compels Mags to walk through the office spraying the staff 'plane-in-malaria-area' style, tell her you've read a report that the average desk surface contains fifty types of bacteria including traces of rat droppings, mouse crap, human hair, vomit, urine, faeces and bodily fluids. She'll be so busy with her disinfectant wipes that her focus will be off you.

Bullying Manager

Brian's tyrannical regime is like a railway station, with the constant coming and going of people, either booted out by Brian or fleeing in terror before he gets to them. Like all dictators, Brian cultivates an atmosphere of fear. He does this by systematically undermining his staff and obliquely threatening them with talk of funding shortages, redundancy and the recession.

Brian's bullying tactics ensure that his staff are too scared, i.e. worried about paying their mortgages to challenge him. If you do summon up the courage, he will subject you to remorseless intimidation. He'll disparage you in meetings, rubbish your work and outline your deficiencies at regular intervals. If you object, he'll tell you not to be defensive. When you retreat into your shell and do a no-show at the Christmas party, Brian will play his trump card and accuse you of not being a team player. You will feel demoralized and your self-esteem will plummet.

Brian is a hypocrite and will discipline staff for things he does all the time. He will make false promises and lie blithely about things he is supposed to have done. He will shout you down in meetings, then tell you not to interrupt him if you attempt to reply. He will lecture you about time management and absence from the office, then fail to turn up to meetings with no explanation. He will randomly change instructions so you are never quite sure what to expect. You might stay up all night finishing work to meet a deadline, but when you flop exhausted into the office the next morning, Brian will tell you he only needs it in five days.

'It's an out of hours memo from my office manager.'

Brian's favourite crap management technique is to keep his staff in a state of uncertainty by playing good cop, bad cop because this reinforces his sense of power. Just when you can no longer bear his bombardment of criticism, he will make a patronizing but slightly complimentary comment about your work. He will order in a box of cookies for the staff – an inviting treat to hide the wickedness, like the gingerbread house in Hansel and Gretel. The cookies will sit on the desk, chocolately and alluring, but don't be tempted to eat one of Brian's treacherous cookies. You will be colluding with the fact that he can treat you like shit most of the time, but all will be forgotten as soon as the warm sweetness hits your palate.

Brian is a psychopath, but unfortunately he can appear quite plausible, and even charming on occasion. He cultivates relationships with the right people, thus creating an enclave of power and influence around himself that is impossible to penetrate. If you try to make an official complaint against Brian, you will slap straight into the wall of his supporters in high places.

TOP TIP

FOR DEALING WITH BRIAN

Brian has a deep-seated personality disorder which makes it really difficult to work for him. If you become unable to stop yourself tweaking his sideburn in a meeting, or you receive some inside information that he's about to sack you, it's time for decisive action. Tell Brian you're going on your lunch break, make sure you take all your personal stuff, and don't come back. Ever. Just before you leave, take the box of cookies, put them on the glass plate of the photocopy machine and slam the lid down on them.

Capitulating Manager

Charles is a bully who deep down is a weak, cowardly person. He puts on a show of strong-arm tactics because he wants to impress senior management. He doesn't have a commanding presence but the hierarchical structure of the office allows him to dish it out by virtue of his post. He has maintained his dominant position by default because disgruntled staff members have always resigned instead of staying and confronting him.

You will be dreading your upcoming appraisal with Charles, because he will use it as an opportunity to flex his petty authority muscles. Before going into Charles's office, you'll receive a phone call to say your mother has had a heart attack. You'll want to rush off to the hospital, but unbelievably, Charles will not let you go until the appraisal is done. In the distant recesses of his brain, a tiny dot of conscience will briefly flicker and he'll say he's sorry for your news, but a moment later he will return to the important matter of whether or not you are contributing in a meaningful way to the development of the organization. You will have to sit there, distracted and upset, while Charles lectures you for not trying hard enough to meet the impossible work targets he has set. Eventually you'll stand up and say: "That's it – I QUIT!"

Actually you won't, that only happens in Hollywood movies. You won't leave because you can't afford to do so, and you are terrified of the dearth of jobs in the recession, but you will resolve to do something. You will start your defensive action by building up ammunition. This will be a pile of books on your desk with titles like 'The Essential Guide to Employees Rights' or 'Fire me and I'll Sue'. On top of the pile will be a large note saying: 'My books about employment law'. You'll scrutinize your job contract to see how many times Charles has violated it, and then arrange a meeting with your beleaguered colleagues to persuade them to take out a collective grievance against Charles. You'll gather after work in a smoky Greek café and plot your revenge over hummus and pitta bread. The next day in the office you'll produce a grievance statement about Charles's unacceptable behaviour, but the bravado of the night before in the Kalamaras café will have faded and everyone will be shitting themselves that they won't be able to pay their credit card bills. The only signatures on the form will be yours and that of Mercy the office cleaner, who thought she was signing up for a free lunch.

But all will not be lost. It will be worth taking out a grievance on your own, because you will be surprised how easily Charles capitulates when challenged. Once you have lodged your grievance with senior management, Charles will be intent on covering his back and making sure the grievance doesn't reveal to his superiors what a crap manager he is. Long before the process reaches an employment tribunal, he will follow the easy route and take long-term sick leave. He'll take out a grievance against the organisation because he's too 'ill' to return to work, and the cause of the grievance will be that his line manager failed to deal properly with the counter-grievance he took out against your grievance in a way that was fair to him.

 **TOP TIP**

FOR DEALING WITH CHARLES

Join a union with a militant, ball-crunching representative from the wrong side of Peckham with big biceps and a sound knowledge of employment law.

SECTION 2
The Bullshit Artists

Consultant Manager

There is a quote by George Bernard Shaw: 'Those who can, do, and those who can't, teach'. This should be changed to: "Those who can, do many useful and fascinating things, and those who can't become management consultants".

Being a management consultant means charging ridiculous amounts of money for giving advice that is basically common sense. Management consultancy has burgeoned into a thriving industry of horseshit because managers are no longer expected to merely have a sound mind and relevant experience. Their work is so 'complicated' it has to be outsourced to management consultants like Campbell. Your manager will consider Campbell's services essential and, at £5000 a day, excellent value for money. You might think that the work done by Campbell should be the responsibility of your manager who has been appointed on a large salary after a rigorous recruitment process. Apparently the fact that he has seen the need to bring in a consultant shows what incredible insight he has as a manager.

There is an abundance of management consultants with

different approaches, but one thing unites them – they are seriously irritating, and Campbell is no exception.

'Well for a management consultant he's refreshingly honest"

During his staff training sessions, you'll be listening to his meaningless cant, thinking: "When's he going to mention that hackneyed old chestnut, the infamous SWOT (Strengths, Weaknesses, Opportunities, Threats) analysis?" Sure enough, he'll trot it out as though it's a brilliant example of contemporary practice, instead of a banal management tool that has been kicking around since Albert Humphrey created it in the 1960s. Campbell's self-satisfied manner will be intensely annoying and you will fantasize about taking his coffee cup out of his hand, pouring it over his head and watching it trickle down his perky beard into his open-necked, pink shirt.

Campbell will waffle on about the 'science of management'. You'll be tempted to tell him that management is not a science, and remind him of the work that real scientists do, like trying to find a cure for cancer or preventing the destruction of the planet from global warming. Tragically Campbell thinks management consultants are more important than scientists. He doesn't realize that if they all disappeared tomorrow, no one would notice or care.

When Campbell presents his final fuzzword-laden report, it will be full of non-specific recommendations to contrived problems with exaggerated assumptions of what can be achieved. If you try and read it, you will lose the will to live by the second paragraph. No normal person will understand how to apply it in the workplace. In the unlikely event that Campbell's report contains the tiniest hint of criticism about your manager, it will never see the light of day. It will be hidden at the back of a filing cabinet gathering dust until another manager comes along and outsources the work to a different management consultant at enormous cost, because Campbell's inflated and mind-bogglingly expensive opus is no longer 'relevant to the operational field in the current climate'.

TOP TIP

FOR DEALING WITH CAMPBELL

If you swallow your cynicism, you could benefit from having to endure Campbell. Take copious notes while he is talking, hang onto his handouts, steal his unoriginal ideas and set up a management consultancy of your own. That way you too could earn money for old rope.

Well-Being Manager

Another crap management theory doing the rounds these days is Workplace Well-being. Managers use it to increase productivity and reduce absenteeism under the guise of caring for staff welfare. Wendy's role in your organisation is to ensure that well-being practices are 'deeply embedded' by training staff how to be nice to each other and to back up their niceness with evidence and paperwork.

Wendy will run a series of workshops on well-being that take crap management to a new level. She will produce a jolly, colourful chart to outline her *Well-Being Planning Strategy*, to show you exactly when and how you have to be nice to your colleagues (hopefully, the earmarked sessions won't fall on the day you have a bad hangover!). In the dictionary, 'well-being' is defined as 'a state of being good, healthy or comfortable'. You will feel none of these things by the time Wendy has finished with you.

Wendy will distribute the Happiness Log, an Excel spreadsheet on which you have to build a library of 'happiness moments', a list of times in the office when your heart sings with joy. Difficult, because happiness is one of those mysterious emotions that evaporates as soon as you think about it, and most normal people don't have bursts of euphoria at work. You might be tempted to quote this old Chinese proverb to Wendy: "Same old slippers, same old rice, same old glimpse of paradise."

Any shred of well-being you have managed to preserve will be shattered after you attend Wendy's 'Laughter is a Serious Business' workshop. This 'hilarious' activity is designed to make staff aware of the benefits of laughing and boost their morale, but like onion tears, fake laughing doesn't psychologically produce the same effect as real laughter. It will be a terrifying experience. You'll find yourself sitting in a circle with your co-workers in a dimly lit room with Wendy laughing like a maniacal hyena. Some of your more malleable colleagues will join in with an embarrassed guffaw, but you'll be stunned into petrified silence. You'll feel traumatised for weeks afterwards, unable to produce even a wry smile.

Once Wendy has outlined her Well-Being Strategy, she will set about implementing it with unrelenting vigour, storming down corridors, poking in every nook and cranny looking for offenders. If she doesn't catch you red-handed, she will leave reminders about your well-being transgressions. If you make yourself a cup of tea in the staff kitchen, don't leave the teabag by the sink. You may have thought this meant you were a scruffy slob with poor housekeeping standards, but Wendy will set you straight. She will leave a yellow post-it on the teabag that says: "This is not good well-being practice." You'll be tempted to stick the post-it on Wendy's forehead, and then open the teabag and scatter the soggy leaves over the counter.

Human beings are delightfully unpredictable which is why they can't be pigeonholed by initiatives and procedures. You may previously have been a reasonable person with a genuine regard for most of your colleagues, but Wendy's well-being agenda will transform you into an embittered, cantankerous, misanthropic individual who hates the human race.

FOR DEALING WITH WENDY

SUGGESTIONS FOR YOUR 'HAPPINESS LOG'	
Day	Reason for feelings of happiness
Fri 5pm	I don't have to go to work for the next two days.
Sat 10am	I don't have to go to work today.
Sun 11am	I don't have to go to work today either.
Wed 12pm	I'm fantasizing that I've won the lottery and won't ever have to go to work again.

JUSTIN

Jargon-Spewing Manager

Justin has recently graduated with an MBA which he did online through a distance learning programme from an American business college. It's impossible to understand a word of the managerial jargon he uses, but you won't dare ask him what 'needs matrix' or 'proof of concept outcomes' mean for fear of appearing thick. Justin's doublespeak is like the duckspeak in Orwell's Nineteen Eighty-Four: "It consisted of words, but it was not speech in the true sense, it was a noise uttered in unconsciousness, like the quacking of a duck."

Justin worships paperwork i.e. needless collection of information. He will inflict his form-filling idolatry on you by demanding voluminous reports on the deliverables, baseline targets, outcomes and outputs of your job. Don't ask him to explain the difference between 'outcome' and 'output' – you'll only feel depressed.

When you see the torturous paperwork Justin wants you to complete, you will be overcome by a tired, swampy sensation, as though you have slipped into a bog from which you can't drag your body.

'I'm the Council's Registered Acronym Promoter but I've yet to be given a job title.'

As part of your job, you have to produce a self-help guide on intervention in domestic violence cases, which you try to make as clear and direct as possible. Justin will put a red pen through it and replace it with his DOVSAP (Domestic Violence Strategic Assessment Plan), a cumbersome, jargon-laden document with mystifying sentences like: "Building in equality assessments, the options are microscoped through the operational land-scape to arrive at an output-based specification." Which will be wonderfully useful when confronting a violent, abusive husband looking for his wife.

Justin adores acronyms – they provide a camouflage for

his deficit of imagination and talent. He adopts a bashful, coy expression when he delivers sentences that hang heavy with them. His personal mantra is SMART which stands for strategic...maybe, or is it specific?... measurable ...accessible? no, achievable?...realistic?...timely, tangible, turgid? - who knows what the hell it means? Justin will talk about SMART in a tone of awed reverence, but you might think of it in a different way: "Stupid Mindless Awful Rubbish To-put-up-with."

During your staff supervision session, Justin will embrace all areas of crap management like asking you what your weaknesses are. Your mind will go blank, and your brain will be scrambling for something to say. Justin will interpret this as a sign of weakness, so just make up any old thing like: "One of my weaknesses is that I want to poke a pencil in my eye when someone at the next desk is loudly eating a packet of crisps." If you admit to a real difficulty, like the fact that you don't understand what the acronyms in Justin's reports stand for, he'll use it against you when he's looking for a staff member to make redundant. You should regard your lack of acronym literacy as a strength not weakness because it shows how insightful you are.

TOP
TIP

FOR DEALING WITH JUSTIN

Write a report full of acronyms. Justin will be unfamiliar with them as you will have made them up. He won't dare admit that he doesn't know what they mean, so he will hire an interpreter.

When he launches into his management-speak feedback, take the document from him, put it in the shredding machine, throw the shredded paper around the room and watch it fly from your finger tips like confetti. Then go off on long-term stress absence. Or LOTSA as Justin calls it.

Diversity Manager

Diversity and equality are essential to safeguard against all forms of discrimination, and to ensure that people who would previously have suffered from prejudice in the workplace can now feel their rights are protected. So you will welcome the appointment of Delia, the Diversity Manager. Until you realize that Delia has certain discriminatory practices of her own. She takes an instant dislike to anybody from New Zealand, Australia, America, Canada, the Channel Islands, South Africa and Bermuda. She's so hell-bent on categorizing and labeling people in the correct way that she highlights their differences and not their common humanity.

Delia will talk enthusiastically about 'embedding inclusive practices into the organisation' and 'widening participation' of different groups, unless they happen to be heterosexual, white, middle-class males. Especially if they are old heterosexual, white, middle-class males. Or, in fact, old anybody. Somehow Delia's diversity agenda has failed to address the fact that currently, the most rampant and unashamed discrimination in the work place is ageism.

You'll be required to attend Delia's Anti-Discrimination and Diversity training, based on her assumption that no one except her has any understanding of these issues. Delia will scan the ten page equal opportunities monitoring form she's made everyone complete and discover that only one person has ticked the 'Asian' box. Delia will tell this woman: "I'm sorry but I know you will feel uncomfortable if there is no one else from your community here", before rushing off and returning with a rather surprised man from the policy department. Never mind that he is from India and the woman is from Pakistan and they share neither language nor religion. As far as Delia is concerned they are both 'Asian', and she can tick the ethnic minorities box.

When Delia brings up disability awareness you will be walking on eggshells, desperately trying to remember the latest, constantly changing terminology. Delia will make you feel as though you are a bad person if you can't remember whether people with sight problems should be referred to as 'vision/visual impaired' or 'people with a vision/visual impairment'. Delia will ask the group to do an exercise on designing an office reception desk that will be suitable for PORGS. You will have absolutely no idea what she is talking about and eventually you will have to ask her. She will tell you: "PORG means Person of Restricted Growth. I think PORG is a lovely word for a little person." Why, you will think, does she consider PORG or 'little person' to be so much better than the derogatory term 'dwarf'?

If you suggest brainstorming some ideas to make the office more accessible to a wheelchair user, Delia will urgently cut you off and tell you not to use the word 'brainstorm', as this will offend epilepsy sufferers. Delia will ask you to say 'thought shower' instead. Apparently people with epilepsy don't make any connection between this and the violent electrical activity that characterizes their seizures. So 'thought shower' it is until it offends someone else. That is why Delia is in permanent employment.

FOR DEALING WITH DELIA

Don't ever say: 'Happy Christmas, Delia.' She will find it deeply offensive. Instead repeat the following:

'Best wishes for the previously pagan forthcoming festive season in particular one day just past the winter solstice on which you may find yourself consuming large amounts of turkey and mince pies.'

Health And Safety Manager

Hamish is great. He is valued in his local community, and volunteers to be a snow warden for his street every winter. So why do you hate him? It's the way he saps the joie de vivre out of even the most optimistic person with his Health and Safety Agenda, which has taken a few necessary precautions to ensure the survival of the human race and translated them into a brave new world of crap management absurdity.

Most of us have to put up with silly health and safety policies and practices at work, but Hamish applies them enthusiastically in his personal life. He actually reads the terms and conditions in insurance policies, instead of just ticking the 'yes' box. Hamish has illuminated strips on the inside door of his Volvo (purchased after a lengthy relationship with Which magazine to determine the car's safety record) so passing traffic will know HE IS OPENING HIS CAR DOOR and won't rip it off as they drive past. If he goes for a walk he wears the correct footwear and a bright yellow Day-Glo jacket so he can be seen clearly. He's oblivious to the occasional white van driver who shouts 'fucking wanker' as they drive past him.

'You can forget work today...some reckless psychopath has dropped a bannana skin.'

You'll find it hard to believe Hamish's marriage has lasted after he's told a few family anecdotes to make his H&S seminars more folksy and accessible. Like how his wife fails to observe health and safety rules when she's cooking chips, because the careless woman doesn't have the fire safety blanket ready to smother the frying pan if the oil catches fire. Hamish will tell you how amusing it is when they go on holiday to Greece, and he doesn't notice the stunning view of the Mediterranean outside his window because he's too busy doing a risk assessment on the hotel room. A mean thought will pop into your head. You will imagine Hamish sitting on his sofa having covered all the health and safety bases, when a random act of God occurs and a heavy picture falls off the wall and onto his head.

Hamish will find potential danger in the most harmless activities. If you bring out your knitting during the lunch break, he will tell you that the cute baby jumper you are making for your infant niece is a risk because of the needles. They may cause an accident in the office. To evaluate this and all other conceivable potential hazards, Hamish will tell you to do a risk assessment. You will produce a reasonable document on being alone in the office or stacking folders on high shelves. Hamish will give you a superior smile and say it is not a proper risk assessment, pronounced with a sibilant 's' that will grate right on your nerves. You will go demented trying to pad out the information until you will want to whack Hamish over the head with your risk assessment folder and shout: "*a life lived in fear is a life half-lived.*"

TOP TIP

FOR DEALING WITH HAMISH

To get rid of Hamish, propose to head office that his impressive health and safety skills shouldn't be confined to the company, but outsourced and implemented in a challenging place where their brilliance can be demonstrated. Like Mogadishu, one of the most dangerous places on earth. A city filled with crumbling buildings pock-marked with bullet holes, burnt out vehicles, piles of garbage, endemic illnesses. It's a perfect post-apocalyptic environment just crying out for Hamish to deliver his seminar on using a stepladder safely.

Quality Assurance Manager

Quentin is the Quality Assurance Manager. Not to be confused with Quality Street chocolates, which have a far more useful function. Quentin has the most pointless job in the universe with an inflated salary that doesn't reflect the futility of his work; if it did he would earn about £5 a week instead of roughly the same as a consultant heart surgeon in a busy NHS hospital.

Quality control is good when used in the right context to ensure that a product or service is fit for purpose and meets certain requirements like legal compliance and customer expectations – in other words, you want to be sure that the x-ray machine is working effectively when it photographs your humerus to see whether you have a fracture. But the bullshitters in career management have hijacked this concept and applied it inappropriately to the public and charity sector to give twats like Quentin an ill-deserved, criminally overpaid employment opportunity.

Every time you walk past Quentin's office, you'll think to yourself: 'What the fuck does he actually do?' After he's told you fifteen times you'll be none the wiser. In a meeting of external stakeholders Quentin will outline his post: "Hi, I'm Quentin, I'm the Quality Assurance Manager, I monitor quality management systems blah blah blah, and produce superfluous bullshit reports on performance against set indicators blah blah." Then a smile will play around his lips as he prepares for a witticism: "I have to 'persuade' reluctant staff to change their way of working to incorporate quality methods." The stakeholders round the table with the same kind of ludicrous job titles as Quentin will titter appreciatively. You'll struggle to stop yourself jumping out the nearest window.

While Quentin is yapping on, you will be unable to prevent your mind from wandering all over the place – off it will go to the shopping mall, the beach at Goa, the steak and chips you are having for dinner and what you would do if you won the lottery. Your attention will switch back to the meeting when someone mentions Picasso. At last something interesting is being discussed, you will think. Will it be the Blue Period, cubism or the fascination of Guernica? But no, it's PQASSO, a quality assurance system designed for charitable organisations who waste precious time and money buying into it, because Quentin has hoodwinked them into believing it is necessary to their development. For instance, a cash-strapped refugee charity without even a functioning photo-copier will drive themselves into the wall trying to fulfill the obligations of PQASSO, taking vital front-line work away from the desperate asylum seekers that pour through their doors.

FOR DEALING WITH QUENTIN

When you are compelled to attend one of Quentin's meetings, use this technique called "Pretending to be interested when Listening to Boring Bullshit". You will appear to be paying attention.

Your eyes will be wide open and fixed on Quentin, but you'll be asleep inside your head. Your brain will be taking little catnaps.

SECTION 3
The Egotists

Narcissistic Manager

Nigel is a relentless self-promoter who believes that the world revolves around him; this is bad news for his staff who are the blameless victims of his crap management. The cornerstones of Nigel's self-belief are the four A's — Admiration, Adulation, Attention and Affirmation — for Nigel.

Nigel is convinced that he has bucket-loads of charisma and everyone is dumbstruck by his statesmanlike presence. He deludes himself that his colleagues regard him as a genius in his field, and will understand when he behaves like a shit, because 'special' people have unpredictable personalities. Or so his psychiatrist tells him.

Nigel mistakenly believes he is indispensable. He manages a small arts charity, but he behaves as though he is running the United Nations. He will walk around the office with a furrowed brow from the weight of the 'crucial' decisions he has to make. If you need to talk to him and spend more than two minutes explaining the issue, he will look pained but imperious. Then he will cut you short because you are wasting the valuable time of such an important person. He will regard you despairingly and say: "But we've already been through this." It would never occur to him that he hasn't communicated the information clearly.

Nigel will be nice to you if you are young and pretty, although the niceness comes at a price, because he will flirt with you in a kind of an indulgent yet intimidating way that will put you off taking out a sexism grievance. Generally, however, he never smiles at his staff during working hours because he believes doing so undermines the professionalism of the organisation.

Nigel doesn't believe in teamwork — it detracts too much from his giant ego. He thinks it is necessary to be dictatorial toward his staff to maintain the mystique of his higher authority. He is the guru and the staff should be his unquestioning followers. Like all narcissists, Nigel is prone to paranoia, so he will appoint a sidekick to 'observe' everybody. The sidekick will spy on the staff by reading emails and listening at doors, giving Nigel information of any potential plans for mutiny among the staff.

Nigel thinks of himself as a high-powered player and he wants to ensure his job title reflects this. Not content with 'manager', he will consider the various options – Managing Director, Director, Artistic Director, Arts Czar, Chief Executive Officer, Big Shot, High Priest, God. He will award himself an accompanying generous salary. His staff will keep their menial salaries and lowly titles like assistant and project worker. This is because Nigel believes it is such a privilege to work with someone of his standing, people should be prepared to do it for peanuts.

TOP TIP

FOR DEALING WITH NIGEL

Nigel is a self-serving idiot who will never change. You need to get the better of him. One way to do this would be to advertise his job in the recruitment section of various newspapers without telling him. Then see his reaction when the prospective applicants start ringing up to enquire about his job.

Retail Manager

Rafael may have left school with only one A-C grade for his GCSEs, but as far as he is concerned, he knows everything about strategic marketing, and represents a new and exciting breed of managers in retail. He made a name for himself transforming a tired, department store cosmetic counter into a million-pound enterprise. He turfed out the senior citizens loitering around the lipstick section looking for a nice colour to match their blue rinse, and replaced them with hordes of gullible people enticed by the offer of a 'free' makeover. Once they had been virtually embalmed by copious amounts of foundation, they were told to spend £200 on beauty products to redeem the cost of the makeover, or they wouldn't be allowed to leave the store. Because of this duplicitous, mendacious marketing ploy – sorry, entrepreneurial success – Rafael has been recruited to bolster the fortunes of make-up and perfumery in your shop on Oxford Street. He will prance into your life every morning, flaunting his fluorescent orange tan and XFactor, boy band quiff, and your job will cease to be enjoyable.

Rafael will constantly beat you over the head with his track record and won't appreciate what he calls your 'customer-centric' approach, which he claims is bad for business. He'll berate you for squandering a perfect sales opportunity by 'wasting' so much time on one customer – the woman who burst into tears and told you that her boyfriend had broken up with her and made her feel unattractive. You gave her a brilliant makeover with some bonus therapeutic advice and she left much happier. Rafael will put a stop to all that, even though your sales figures have always been good precisely because of your genuine interest in the customers.

Rafael will allocate you a metre of space and instruct you not stray over an invisible line into another beauty adviser's area. That way he can tell which staff member is raking in the biggest profit. He will insist you follow his rigid retail format, one of the cornerstones of his success; you will be required to repeat a set mantra of sales patter, designed to entice the customer into buying something they don't need or want. The customers will lose interest before you have finished speaking, your sales targets will plummet, and Rafael will become concerned.

When Rafael goes on a training course, you happily drop the format, chatting to the customers about their children and what the type of mascara suits them. You'll have a great time but a few days later a registered letter will be delivered to your house by courier telling you to attend a disciplinary meeting at head office. While Rafael was pratting about on his Career Progression in Supervisory Management Training Course called 'How to be an Even Bigger Fish in a Very Small Pond', he arranged for the counter to be visited by a mystery shopper. This person was from head office pretending to be a customer to entrap the staff (you might remember the rude French woman who couldn't decide which eye cream to buy). She reported that you didn't follow the format. Shock! Horror! After this, Rafael will be on your case constantly. He'll tell you off about trivial matters, loudly, in front of customers. You'll feel like a caged animal in your allotted area, confined to an invisible prison, albeit a fragrant one. You'll realize that the smell of perfume gives you a headache.

 **TOP TIP**

FOR DEALING WITH RAFAEL

Select one of the more expensive designer lipsticks, and use it to write 'So long, I'm off to star in a West End show' in big letters across the cosmetic mirror on the counter. Then sweep out of the shop, and disappear into the crowds on Oxford Street.

Funky Manager

Fenella calls herself Fen for short and she is funky! She owns a television production company and is fabulous, hilarious and hip to everyone except her staff. For them, she doesn't bother with the 'funky' stuff – she treats them like shit.

Fen's life is cosseted by inherited wealth. She can do whatever she chooses – become a media mogul, have her house decorated in rose petals flown in from Lithuania, or pay £2000 for her wardrobe to be sorted into co-ordinated colours by a company called the Wardrobe Fairies. You'll be surprised Fen employs someone to do this, because your own twelve-year-old daughter has done so since she was eight. Fen's financial blessings mean that she has no concept of how money determines life decisions. When you tell her that you have to move out of your flat while the damp is being treated, she will recommend a hotel where a double room costs £1000 a night.

According to Fen, she is well known for her fantastic people skills. Unfortunately you won't benefit from them unless you are a celebrity or fabulously rich. The moody, off-hand demeanour she presents to her staff will change the moment she receives a phone call from one of her celebrity connections. She'll rush off to have lunch with a famous media personality and you'll have to look suitably impressed. Then gobble your lunch while she's out because Fen hates food smells, other than her daily dose of calorie-free edamame beans and jasmine tea.

'We need some sweets in reception - use this colour chart.'

Fen shudders at mediocrity – it makes her so sad. Her production company must be the 'craziest and best' place to work. Not to those who actually work there but important visitors. Fen will have the doors painted in different colors – a cacophony of red, green, yellow and pink. Such fun, Fen will declare! You'll be obliged not to resent the cramped space you share with eight colleagues because the door is a rich shade of magenta. Fen's vast, cavernous room will be a testament to love – the love she has for herself – with 'Fen's Inner Sanctuary' emblazoned in pink neon lights and delicate blasts of tea rose wafting through the air. Dotted around the office will be bowls of sweets which have been selected to recreate images of yesteryear – the 1950s are so in – jelly babies, gob stoppers, sherbet sizzlers and pink sugared mice. Sounds delicious, but unfortunately they're not for the staff. Just as you pop a liquorice allsort into your mouth, Fen will loom up and smack the sweet out of your hand.

Your ultimate humiliation will come when the office is visited by some television-commissioners Fen is determined to dazzle. Fen will be worried that the psychedelic doors and jellybeans won't be enough to impress them; a scene of wanton creativity will also be required. She will instruct the staff to leap up and dance 'spontaneously' around the office at a given signal. Poor old paunchy Stan from accounts will be flailing about like an asthmatic bear and you'll be self-consciously jigging up and down thinking that death is not such a bad option. When the visiting delegation appears at the door, Fen will come dancing out of her office like a bat on speed, big sunglasses perched on her taut, botoxed face, 47 going on 30. "Wow," the visitors will say. "It must be amazing to work here."

FOR DEALING WITH FEN

If she catches you with traces of white powder around your mouth, tell her it's cocaine and she won't mind a bit. But if she finds out you've actually helped yourself to a sherbet sizzler from the forbidden sweetie tray, you'll be in deep shit.

SECTION 4
The Lazy Gits

Can't-Do-Her-Job Manager

Carroll has landed herself a management post in your organization, a job for which she is ill-equipped i.e. she has neither the requisite qualifications nor experience. Carroll didn't acquit herself very well in her interview, but the rest of the candidates were even worse. The company couldn't be bothered to re-advertise, so Carroll slipped right through the net and into your life. You won't be under any illusions about her incompetence because this will be revealed when she asks blatantly ill-informed questions that someone in her management position should know. Carroll is also bloody lazy, as you will discover.

When she first arrives, she will pretend to work very hard by staying in the office after six o'clock, while you will be plodding home at the normal time. But then she will start ladling her job duties onto her competent staff team. As she delegates more and more (i.e. shoves her work onto some other poor bastard), you'll find yourself working longer hours, leaving the office later in the evening. At the same time Carroll will begin leaving earlier – her hours will diminish as yours increase. You will feel stressed by your enormous workload, and annoyed to find yourself doing her job, when she is paid considerably more than you are. But if you object, Carroll will pull you up for attitude problems.

Carroll may know nothing about her job but she possesses a cunning intelligence for maintaining the pretense of being a good manager. She will perform her 'I'm so exhausted and over-loaded with work' routine whenever her line manager is around. The deception works because Carroll will be .showered with praise and described as 'the hardest working manager we've had for a long time'.

She will take credit for everyone else's hard work. You might spend six months putting in overtime to organize a corporate event, then you'll overhear Carroll saying to one of her senior managers: "Yes, it has been a lot of work and I'm absolutely knackered but it was worth it. I couldn't have done it without the support of my colleagues." In this way she manages to convey the impression that she did all the work and yet she's gener-ously giving her minions some of the credit.

Carroll will probably end up with an OBE at some point in her career and you know what that stands for: Other Bugger's Efforts.

TOP TIP

FOR DEALING WITH CARROLL

The next time Carroll makes you write a report for which you know she will take credit, be creative. She will assume it is done to your usual high standard, so will put her name at the top and email it to all her contacts without reading it. Unfortunately for her, everyone else will read it and discover 'Carroll's' glaring faux pas. 'She' consis-tently will have referred to one of the most important investors as Mr Shit Pooh instead of his real name, Mr Shi Poon.

Goofing-Off Manager

You might wonder sometimes if Glyn exists. Only the indentation on the seat pad of his leather swivel chair indicates that someone has been there. Glyn will find any excuse to leave the office. He will attend training courses that are irrelevant to his job like 'Raising Awareness of Breast-feeding among Migrants from Ecuador' when he manages a local authority department responsible for parking fines, clamping and towing.

Glyn loves conferences because they present him with perfect goofing-off opportunities. He will arrive at the conference, grab the information pack, do around ten minutes of networking (enough for people to remember they've seen him there), then slink off to the nearest pub. He'll creep back at four o'clock to take notes, so he has something concrete to produce when he reports to his staff team.

Glyn always hides in his office, playing with his butt station desk tidy. He's petrified of face-to-face communication with the staff, so he will email you instead – pointless, repetitive emails that are a pathetic attempt to make it look like he is doing some work. If you want to scare Glyn, corner him when he comes out the toilet, and tell him earnestly that you want to schedule a two-hour meeting to discuss 'concerns' about your job.

'This is our manager who prides himself on being very much *hands off.*'

Glyn has perfected a technique of looking busy at his desk so that no one can ask him to do anything. The office could be stormed by a furious, axe-wielding man who has received a fine between parking his car and walking the twenty metres to the ticket machine, but Glyn will be unable to deal with it because he is taking an 'important' phone call. Glyn's right hand is glued permanently to the phone. Sometimes he is actually talking to someone but often there is no one on the other end of the line. Glyn knows that as soon as he puts the phone down he will have to do some work. The office will be heaving with problems that he should address, and you will be tempted to put a drawing pin on his swivel chair to galvanise his fat arse into action.

It will be difficult to confront Glyn about not doing his job. He calls his management style 'hands off', which apparently 'empowers his staff'. Unfortunately, the person in the appropriate position to challenge Glyn i.e. his line manager, is just as incompetent and lazy. He knows that if he exposes Glyn, he'll be in the firing line himself for ignoring Glyn's obvious shortcomings, and failing to remove him from his post. He doesn't want the poor judgment that led to Glyn's appointment to reflect on him, especially as he was on the interview panel. So it is in his interests to keep referring to Glyn as an 'asset to the organisation'.

 **TOP TIP**

FOR DEALING WITH GLYN

If Glyn can't be bothered to do his job, why should you care about yours? He gets paid a lot more than you for doing fuck-all. Go with the flow. Take long lunches; make idle chitchat with your colleagues; flood your Twitter account with brilliant soundbites; check your Facebook to see the latest trite aphorism on your newsfeed; set a new record for Solitaire.

SECTION 5
The Work Addicts

Childfree Manager

Chayla has decided not to have children for the sake of her career and loathes staff members with kids. If you have two or three, you will be doomed. Chayla can't see why she should have to sacrifice family life for her career, when you waltz in with splats of baby puke on your jumper and still manage to maintain a reasonably good role in the company? Don't raise the issue of family-friendly policies at meetings, unless you want a lecture from Chayla about people without children who also have needs, like important 'me time' at the yoga retreat.

Chayla works twelve-hour days and will look annoyed if you leave at six o'clock. She never takes her lunch hour. She will bring food from home, and won't even spend ten minutes sitting back in her chair with her feet up. Instead, she will continue to tap away at the computer, peering intently at the screen to let everyone know she is not taking time off for lunch. Now and then she will take small, rabbit nibbles at her food before putting it down for another ten minutes. The reason Chayla can act with such restraint despite the delicious, bready smell wafting tantalizingly up her nostrils, is that she has turned dysfunctional workaholism into a virtue. If you take your full lunch hour, Chayla will make oblique comments about how she wishes she could take time off for a nice long lunch. Ironically, because you have had a break from work you will have a far more productive afternoon than Chayla, whose brain will go into meltdown.

Chayla emails staff members at three in the morning and comes into the office on weekends. She has no comprehension of Saturdays and Sundays being spent dealing with the minutiae of family life, the feeding and entertaining of children, the general chaos. Chayla won't realize what a miracle it is that you turn up to work on a Monday morning. If you appear tired during the working day or burst into tears because your child is being bullied at his nursery school by a smarmy kid called Joshy, Chayla will bring up your lack of focus during supervision. Chayla has no children, so she hasn't learnt that salutary lesson that is forced on parents – a sense of perspective.

If she changes her mind and has children at a later stage in her career, (after much planning about the strategic time to do so) she'll make damn sure they don't affect her work commitments. Chayla will devote time to her children. She will spend time organizing their lives into feeding, playing and bedtime schedules, which will be executed with military precision by a well-paid nanny. Chayla has nothing but contempt for those 'untidy' parents who allow themselves to be taken over by their children's lives.

TOP TIP

FOR DEALING WITH CHAYLA

If your child wakes up one weekday morning with a burning fever, and you don't want to leave him with the childminder, this is what you do. Do not under any circumstances let Chayla know you have a sick child. Ram some wads of tissue up your nose, phone Chayla and when she answers, push your voice into the back of your throat and make that croaky, gurgling noise that people do when they are imitating a motorbike. Tell her that you have tonsillitis.

Iron Constitution Manager

Irene has a bad case of office presenteeism. This is the opposite of absenteeism and refers to people who continue to come to work even if they have only ten hours to live. Irene can't see why you should have to miss work when there are aids such as portable oxygen machines and ambulatory ECG testers. When you hear her boast how she's never had a day off sick in the last ten years, you'll know that falling ill is not an option.

Irene believes that if she takes time off work she is setting a bad example to her staff team. If she catches the flu, she will heavily medicate herself and stagger into work with a rattling chest and a voice like a frog being strangled. She will have an air of martyred suffering that will make you want to punch her mottled red nose. When you bring her a cup of tea, she will drink it with her hand fluttering in front of her throat, as if trying to hold in her tonsils while she swallows with difficulty.

If you suggest that she would be better off in bed, she will smile weakly and say: "Oh I couldn't possibly, there is so much to do here." She will cough and sneeze without restraint, depositing viral microbes all over the office, which will infect the staff touching door handles and other hard surfaces. When they fall ill and stay at home nursing high fevers and thumping head-aches, they won't receive any sympathy from Irene. She will be profoundly disappointed, especially after all the trouble she took to set them a shining example of fortitude and stoicism.

Irene can almost tolerate it if you take an hour off to have an exploding dental abscess treated, but if you take the whole day, you will be subjected to sideswipes about sickness records. Irene will blame your 'excessive absenteeism' on everything that goes wrong in the office. She is a great advocate of the Bradford Factor Index, a tool for monitoring rates of staff sick-ness, invented by someone with a stupid job title and too much spare time. It has a silly formula, SxSxD and a Point's Table to impress managers like Irene. When Irene wants to tackle you about sickness she will bring out her BFI — if you score under 40, your job is safe. If you score between 50 and 100, Irene will find someone else to blame for office problems, under 300, you'll probably still be there the following week, but over 400 ... you're screwed!

As soon as it dawns on you that you can't get sick, your body will start ailing. You will spend your time under Irene's leadership constantly fighting off sniffles, looming sore throats, searing headaches, lumps, bumps and infections. You might never have suffered a migraine, but one day at work you will find yourself with a headache so blinding you'll feel as though your skull will crack if you blink. Don't tell Irene you have a migraine. As far as she is concerned, a migraine has no med-ical basis; it is a malady for malingerers. Contrive a meeting outside the office and crawl off home, clutching your head.

'I hope you're aware of the impact this this has had on our staff and absenteeism record!'

FOR DEALING WITH IRENE

Next time you feel peaky, come into work with a Beijing Special Avian Flu mask. Tell Irene that you have a contagious virus and need to be quarantined. Once you're happily ensconced in the office supplies room, you can settle yourself in a comfortable position with your lozenges and Vicks and doze away. Don't forget to spread your work in front of you to give the impression of being busy in case Irene drops by to check on you.

Section 6
The Great Pretenders

Education Manager

Edwin is a headteacher, but not one who knows all the parents by their first names and cares about the welfare of the pupils. He won't be visited by former pupils for years after they have left school, because he made such a difference to their lives. Edwin doesn't even like children. He hasn't been in a classroom since he was a pupil himself, or worked as a teacher, which is the normal route for headteachers. Fortunately it's not an important aspect of his job, because Edwin isn't a headteacher in the traditional sense of the word — he's a Chief Executive. And a fast-tracked one at that. It wasn't so long ago that Edwin was hot-desking at a merchant bank in the city waiting for a call about his redundancy, when, hey presto, before you could say 'superhead', he found himself in charge of three primary schools. A cluster of schools known as a federation, with Edwin sitting at the top on a big, comfy CEO salary of £200,000. Who says teaching doesn't pay?

Edwin is a lucky recipient of the Government's 'vision' that school management has been hijacked for too long by idealistic educators and should be handed to those who really know how to get things moving – the business sector. Apparently the qualities you need to survive the cutthroat, cocaine-fuelled, merciless striving for supremacy of the financial district are ideal for running schools. As far as the Government is concerned, headteachers, I mean, CEOs, like Edwin are saviours of education management.

Edwin will be a bit bored with just being the CEO of his three schools, so he will arrange for a consultancy with an education policy think-tank, which will take up a significant portion of his time. If you are a teacher in one of Edwin's schools, you probably won't see him much or ever really. The most common sighting will be his car disappearing out the school gates to his think-tank meetings. One of the few times you'll see him, is when you're forced to attend his PowerPoint presentation outlining the *Education Revolution*, reflecting a trail of excellence straight from the Square Mile.

You probably went into teaching to have a safe career; it might not pay well, but it's a job for life, and it offers a pension to keep you in pottery classes and French lessons during your declining years. Under Edwin's leadership none of that is guaranteed. For the first time in your career you will be given a temporary contract; Edwin will want the option to dump you if necessary. You will have to enter a bidding war for your salary, competing with other teachers to prove your worth. Edwin's salary won't be affected by league tables, but yours will if you don't reach your Key Stage SATS attainment targets in English, Maths and Science, even though you have a class where English is the second language of fifty per cent of the pupils. The children will become a minor part of your day. You will be inspected to within an inch of your life, and your good track record will be ignored. Edwin will tell the staff that they are failing and you will have to work sixteen hours a day and through your holidays to remedy these 'failures'. It's part of Edwin's mission, because he's a Government secret agent, not in the MI5 sense, but more of an envoy sent to activate the Government's covert operation to fail all schools and turn them into privately-funded academies, the brave new world of crap education management.

It won't be long before the teachers in Edwin's schools are dropping like flies. You'll find yourself waking in the small hours with a racing heart and a feeling of dread. Then you'll visit the GP to be signed off for stress like the rest of your colleagues.

TOP TIP

FOR DEALING WITH EDWIN

Get 'pit-bull mum' on the case. Tell her that Edwin has given one of her seven kiddies a detention. When he comes back from his education think tank meeting with a nice takeaway chai tea latte in his hand, she'll be waiting for him with her huge tattooed arms and foul mouth.

Her muscled dog will be straining on the leash to have a go at Edwin's designer trousers.

PAUL

Pilfering Manager

Pilfering from an organisation is a serious crime. Officially it is known as embezzling and is the act of taking money that has been placed in your trust but doesn't belong to you. When you work in the same government department as Paul (thin face with mildly annoying moustache), you won't suspect him of anything other than being a nerd – well, he is an accountant and Head of Finance. It won't cross your mind that he might have his hand in the cookie jar.

One day the staff will be called to a 'serious' meeting with the chief executive. Paul will be seated beside him as they outline a matter of grave concern: certain items have gone missing from the office and they suspect they have been stolen. A laptop, a box of printer ink and a bottle of champagne have simply vanished. The management will be determined to get to the bottom of it and all the staff will be interviewed in Paul's office. While Paul is interrogating you, a hot flush will creep across your face, creating two shiny red spots on your cheeks. You will feel an overwhelming guilt, convinced that Paul is giving you a piercing look because he knows it was you. When you see him in the office after that you won't be able to meet his eye, even though the thefts occurred when you were on annual leave. This is because Paul has skillfully deflected the pilfering spotlight away from himself by projecting his guilt onto someone else, and you will have imbibed it by a process called secondary guilt transference.

Sooner or later pilferers get caught, usually when they become greedy and raise the stakes of their thieving. Paul will start off with the laptop and printer ink (the disappearance of the champagne will never be explained), but soon he'll move to 'adjusting his spreadsheets' or cooking the books. Problems will arise over a government apprenticeship scheme to ease youth unemployment. Money will come into your department to run the scheme, and, according to Paul's accounts, will have been spent, but no apprentices will be evident. Not one spotty, idle youth on Jobseeker's Allowance will have been dragged from his Xbox 360 and forced to turn up late on a building site to annoy the staff in a construction company.

Paul will not be able to provide evidence that his project has been delivered and the head of the department will eventually become suspicious. The auditors will be called in and it won't be long before the looting trail leads straight to Paul's door. Several meetings will take place behind closed doors and the office will be humming with gossipy speculation. Eventually the police will arrive and invite Paul to accompany them to the station. Probably not the best time to ask him when your travel expenses will be paid.

'I just wish he wasn't so blatant about the office pilfering.'

FOR DEALING WITH PAUL

Make sure that these words are recorded in every report you write: "Here's my report but I can't complete the finance section as that is not my department and I have no information on how the finances break down. None whatsoever. Sorry, who's Paul?"

Section 7
The Youth Exploiters

Volunteer Manager

Valerie makes shed-loads of money from her online business, using a simple strategy to reap financial rewards. She has a team of staff to do all the work but, and this is sheer genius, she doesn't pay them.

Valerie's company is not based in a developing country exploiting the labour of destitute, starving people. It is in West London taking advantage of university graduates who can't find a paid job. Valerie doesn't call them volunteers. They are interns, so much more prestigious-sounding, conjuring up an image of a placement in Whitehall or Washington, before embarking on a distinguished political career.

When you are swimming in that perilous sea between university and your first job, Valerie will know how to bait the hook and reel you in. If you have recently completed an English degree and are ready to embark on a career in journalism, you will spot Valerie's strategically placed job ad. in a quality newspaper.

It will be worded in such a way as to imply that the successful candidate will have their own regular column in a broadsheet. You'll dazzle Valerie in your interview with all your A's, A*'s and Cambridge First. She'll be excited about having your brains to generate more profits. Not that you'll see any because you'll be a volunteer, I mean, intern. When Valerie hires you, you'll imagine you have won a place at her table in the face of stiff competition. I say table because that is where you will find yourself, sitting with a bunch of other mugs, sorry, interns, in Valerie's kitchen, doubling up as an office. One of the ways Valerie saves money, apart from not paying her skivvies, is to run her business from home.

Valerie will have no scruples about the extent to which she exploits your time and free labour. She'll expect the same level of commitment and professionalism as if she was paying you an attractive salary with benefits. The fantastic career opportunities she's promised will turn out to be nothing more than telephone cold-calling and writing penny-pinching suggestions for the cheapskates that subscribe to her web-site.

Valerie's dot.com company is aimed at stingy people with a short arm and long pocket. It gives them advice on how to be even more tight-fisted with their miserable money. Valerie will take tips from her own web-site, which won't be good news for staff perks. You will be offered a free lunch but, whilst Valerie's fridge is stuffed with home deliveries from a prestigious food hall, your food will be sourced from the special offers shelf of a European discount supermarket chain — frozen pizzas with weird toppings and radioactive orange squash from an unidentifiable country with strange hieroglyphic writing on the Tetrapak carton. The cheap coffee/chicory blend allocated for your use will taste like sugary water. You will need to bring your own toilet roll, unless you want to grate your arse with the hard, shiny paper provided.

'And this is where you'll be for the duration of your internment... I mean internship.'

If you're working around Christmas you'll be in for a treat. Valerie will pull out all the stops for the festive season. She'll hand you a gift in wrapping paper so cheap that your fingers will pop through as you receive it. Inside will be a pair of horrible 'four pairs for a quid' socks. You'll have to feign gratitude, when you will really want to throw the present down and stamp on it.

TOP TIP

FOR DEALING WITH VALERIE

If Valerie goes out, you can forage in her fridge for delicacies. With the tip of your finger, scrape some of the delicious cream cheese icing off the deli carrot cake. When you've had enough, smooth it over with a knife. Valerie will never notice unless you've been too greedy and left bald patches on top of the cake.

Summer Camp Manager

During your GAP year as a team leader on a summer camp in the wilds of Alaska, you may have thought the biggest threat would be a large black bear lumbering through the woods towards your tent. But there will be something far more terrifying to deal with, and it won't be Sarah Palin. Nor will it be the subarctic oceanic climate, volcanoes or glacier ice peaks. The greatest test of your survival skills will be working for Seb the summer camp manager.

Firstly you will need earplugs unless you want to suffer permanent hearing loss, because Seb bellows rather than speaks, and you will find yourself reaching for an invisible remote control to turn the sound down. If he wants to reprimand you for not dragging the children up the hiking trail fast enough, he won't call you into his office for a quick chat. He'll catch sight of you on the other side of the river and yell across the water at you, so that everyone will know that he thinks you're a lazy bastard who doesn't deserve to be there. As far as Seb is concerned, anyone who is standing still (even for a second) and not shouting, leaping or gyrating is not doing their job.

If your significant experience of deep sea diving consists of poodling about your local swimming pool with a snorkel bought from the beach shop on your last seaside holiday, you'd better make yourself scarce. Seb will want you to leap into the ocean headfirst and not stop until you have reached the bottom. Seb's staff induction programme will include abseiling, white-water rafting and sea kayaking. If your kayak flips over and your lungs fill with water, don't cling to the side and cry, because Seb will tell you not to be pathetic and to STOP WHINING.

Seb will never say anything positive about your work. You might spend a week successfully containing a group of children with behavioral problems, but Seb will ignore this and pick on a tiny irrelevance like one of your charges not making their bed properly. He will only be nice to you on changeover day when a new set of kids arrive with their parents, and he gives his introductory pep talk which he finishes by shouting: "K...E...E...P BEING FABULOUS!" But once the parents have waved their children goodbye and their cars have disappeared over the horizon in a cloud of volcanic dust, Seb will revert to his normal charmless self.

You will find out why Seb is such a jerk when you go into his office one day when he's not there. While you're waiting for him, something on his desk will catch your eye. It will be his 'Young People at Work Management Handbook', his source of inspiration, his bible, without which he could not survive. To improve staff performance the book gives managers the following advice: "Young people in the workplace are lazy, overconfident, narcissistic little brats, who think the world owes them a living. To stop them getting above themselves, keep them in a permanent state of confusion and insecurity as to whether they are doing a good job."

TOP TIP

FOR DEALING WITH SEB

Appropriate his Management Handbook from his office, and send him a ransom note saying that unless he starts treating the staff like human beings, the book will be flung into the bottomless depths of the Bering Strait.

Section 8
The Unaware

.

Teenage Manager

Terry isn't a teenager, but he's not long past being one. He is 23 years old and through a lucky combination of nepotism and misplaced sense of entitlement, has landed himself a management job in your office. His pin-striped suit might not fit him, pooling a bit around the ankles, but he is very sure of himself. He has a scary young person's confidence that comes from knowing nothing with no sense of perspective gained from life's hard knocks. Socially, Terry doesn't spend time with people outside the age range of 19-30, although he will tell you that he is dating an 'older' woman. You imagine this to be someone 40-ish but further investigation tells you that she is 30. In the uber-trendy block of flats where Terry lives in East London, a warning bell rings if someone over that age enters the building. As far as he is concerned, he is surprised if a 45-year-old still has their own teeth. As for people over 50, he treats them all as though they are suffering from Vascular Dementia.

If you are around 50 years old, you might feel that you have a great deal to contribute to your job. Your kids are older, so you're not constantly torn between the demands of work and home. You don't have to rush away from your desk after a phone call from your child's primary school to say they are vomiting into their colouring book, or take time off when the child minder goes on holiday. You have wisdom gained from years of experience, have learned to be diplomatic and considered in your reactions, and you have a wealth of acquired skills to bring to the table. You are probably looking forward to Terry coming to you for advice, and valuing your input until you have your performance appraisal with him. That's when you'll realize you are a pathetic waste of space who should have gone to live in the country with your ginger cat waiting for a suitable day when you can just die quietly, so that you don't inconvenience anyone who may have to look after you beyond your sell-by date.

Terry won't directly accuse you of being too old (he doesn't dare because of equal opportunities legislation), but he will make oblique comments that employees over 45 shouldn't be given challenging pieces of work, as their diminishing intellects and failing energy won't be able to cope. He will tell 'funny' age-related stories about his mum, how she always loses her glasses and doesn't understand letters from the bank. You'll stop laughing when you realize his mum is younger than you. If Terry wants to show you something on the computer, he will speak S.L.O.W.L.Y and LOUDLY to help your poor useless self understand the 'complicated' technology.

If there is anyone in the office approaching pension age, they need to yank out their stray grey hairs and get busy with botox. And hide their Freedom Bus Pass. Because if Terry discovers a staff member he can legitimately put out to grass, before they know it, they'll be on the street with their carriage clock wondering what to do with the rest of their life. That's when they can bring out their bus pass – for the journey home.

TOP TIP

FOR DEALING WITH TERRY

The next time Terry makes an ageist comment, lightly mention the Equalities Act 2010 and quote this from Theodore Roosevelt (you might have to explain who that is): "The only time you really live fully is from 30 to 60. The young are slaves to dreams; the old servants of regrets. Only the middle-aged have all their five senses in the keeping of their wits."

Raunchy Manager

Remy's modus operandi in the work place includes flirting, innuendo and a touch of mild perviness. This used to be the case with men bosses, but the lifting of the glass ceiling means you can now expect the same behavior from some women managers. Remy won't complain about inequality at work; she enjoys flirting her way to the top, even if it means acting in a skittish fashion and pretending to be less intelligent than she is.

Remy refers to everything as 'sexy'. You may be bored senseless by reading the minutes from the previous meeting, but when Remy calls them 'sexy', you will see them in a new light, as when you make a suggestion for the forthcoming AGM and Remy applauds it for being 'a really sexy proposal'. You will realize that nothing has changed - Confucius thought that one of the central social problems of his time was that people misused words.

Remy sees her choice of clothes as an important weapon. When she sashays out the door in a mini skirt and fishnet tights, you know she has a meeting outside the office, and there will be men around the table. Remy will visit a rival organization and come back with all their confidential policies and planning records. This is because the person she was seeing was a man, and as Remy crossed and uncrossed her fishnet-clad legs, the poor fool sat there spellbound, lost his power of reasoning and handed over more than he should have. Remy will return to the office with a fake wide-eyed innocence, amazed at how helpful everybody is.

'To give her credit she doesn't just flirt with success.'

When Remy is on the prowl no male will escape. If the IT man comes to fix the computer he will mysteriously disappear for part of the day, and you'll be muttering about the useless British workforce, then you'll find out that Remy has taken him out to lunch. He will be one of many – the lift repairman, the building supervisor, the postman. Although her preference will be young, handsome interns, even the retired IT volunteer with his tweed jacket, greasy hair and scruffy grey beard will not be immune from Remy's smouldering gaze and tinkling laugh.

You'd have to be exceptionally unobservant not to notice how differently she treats the male staff from the rest of you. The men in the office will have an easy ride. If they turn up halfway through the morning Remy will not comment, but if you arrive five minutes beyond nine o'clock, she will bollock you for your 'punctuality' issue. Remy will be hyper-critical of your performance, whereas the men will be allowed to get away with all sorts of slapdash work.

One of the more enlightened men won't welcome being the object of Remy's desire. He'll be so desperate that he will invent an ingenious way to ward off her advances. He won't bath for a few days and will come in wearing dirty, stained clothes covered in dog hair. He'll mush up his desk into a messy heap of papers, files, uneaten pizza and a glass of old, smelly milk. It won't have the desired effect. Remy will glide in and say silkily: "All the men I like have untidy desks."

TOP TIP

FOR DEALING WITH REMY

Play Remy at her own game. Turn up to meetings flaunting your assets and outstrip hers in the process. You might not have aired them publicly since you were breast-feeding, but it's time to be brazen. Put on your Wonderbra with its sexy, see-through, animal print gel cups and add to the effect with a jersey top that has shrunk in the wash. Strut into the room with a cleavage to rival Katie Price's fifth boob and enjoy the annoyance that flashes across Remy's face.

Section 9
The Good Eggs

Haunted Middle Manager

You may have thought that most people regard you as a likeable, helpful person with plenty of friends, so it will come as a shock to find yourself in a position where everyone appears to despise you. This will happen because you have made the dreadful decision to enter that employment abyss, middle management, stuck between the staff team you manage and the management hierarchy above you. What a miserable place to be with no control over your own situation at work or the fortunes of the organisation; responsibility without the hefty compensation and benefits enjoyed by senior management. Contrary to popular misconceptions about being lonely at the top, middle management is the loneliest place.

Your own experience of crap managers will make you want to be supportive to your team, and have a good working relationship, especially as you are stuck together in a small office. To show what a listening, caring manager you are, you will agree to take the concerns of your staff team to senior management, who will be annoyed that you have allowed your staff to have such a strong voice, as they brought you in to do their dirty work and crack the whip. The layers of crappy management above you will stamp on your good intentions.

All this might be bearable if you were assured of the full support of your team, and in an ideal world that would be the case. Some of them will support you in a half-arsed way but they won't be suitably appreciative of the extent to which you have put yourself on the line defending them. They will continue bitching and carping, and there will be no stopping them now that you have encouraged them to air their views, which will wind up senior management even more, and your life will be hellish. After staying awake all night with stress-induced insomnia, you will organize a mediation meeting to resolve the situation, but the whole thing will backfire horribly. Senior management will act all heavy-handed and bollock the staff, who will blame you, and you will be left hanging out to dry.

After that, your colleagues will stop talking as soon as you walk into the room. Never mind being sent to Coventry – try Siberia. You won't know who to trust any more. This will even affect your relationships outside work. You will look at your friends and wonder: "Do they really like me?...do I like them?... are they going to stab me in the back?" You'll be trapped between the 'bitch, bitch, bitch' of your colleagues and the 'bad manager, bad manager' finger-pointing from your superiors. You'll feel weepy and desolate and soon you'll be off to your GP for a comforting course of anti-depressants and a referral to the counselor who will tell you that she has seen three middle managers that week.

TOP TIP

FOR DEALING WITH MIDDLE MANAGEMENT

Don't do it! Life's too short. Unless you're prepared to do the bidding of the managers above you without question, the effect on your health won't be worth it. Take stress leave (everyone does these days), and spend some time at home eating chocolates and talking to your dog while you reassess your life. When you have recovered your equilibrium, go and open a bookshop in Rome.

Odorous Manager

Owen stinks! Not as a manager, he is a genuine, lovely manager. He listens to his staff, takes their concerns on board and lets them have time off when necessary. He is absolutely devoted to the charity for which he works, and he spends long hours doing funding applications to ensure its survival. No, Owen actually does smell. He's the B.O. of the N.G.O.

You'll notice Owen's odour even before you get up close to him. The first time you go to his office, you'll be aware of a musty smell, like the lingering fug that pervades a room after someone has copiously farted. In fact you will immediately suspect that Owen has been blasting away a few silent but violent farts. But whenever you subsequently visit the room that smell will be there, so you will realize that is can't be down to poor old Owen farting all day. That the problem lies within the microbiological complexities that constitute Owen's personal physiology. Due to a dysfunctional digestive system, the smell of his sweat is mighty strong and his breath is pure halitosis.

Come on... you can't all have hayfever in the middle of winter.'

When you sit next to Owen in a meeting you will get the full effect. As he raises his arms behind his head and leans back in his chair, a warm blast of underarm body odour will blow in your direction, making your nostrils pinch together. Not even spraying a can of anti-perspirant would eliminate it. But the real killer is the halitosis. When Owen opens his mouth to speak, his breath will make your eyes water. But you'll have to keep standing there pretending to listen, when you would rather run out the room holding your nose.

But life being life, and because you know Owen can't do anything about it, you'll feel sorry for him and put up with his scent. You'll perfect a few survival techniques like standing some way off and silently ordering your olfactory sensors to shut down. But sooner or later a bitchy employee will make an official complaint about Owen's body odour, and he'll be summoned to Human Resources. Who knows what they expect him to do about it – he can hardly jack up his performance indicators to solve the matter.

A problem like that doesn't go away (or blow away) and there is very little tolerance for people like Owen in the world obsessed with streamlined managers. Sooner or later Owen will be right-sized, fumigated or 'transferred' to another office.

 **TOP TIP**

FOR DEALING WITH OWEN

Poor Owen will be devastated after Human Resources have told him why he is being moved from the office. This is when you need to offer him your support and thank him for being such a great manager.

Great Manager

Read this with caution! Don't raise your hopes! Managers like Genevieve exist only in your wildest dreams.

There are many reasons why Genevieve is not a crap manager. She doesn't have a narcissistic personality disorder. She doesn't have body issues, relationship problems, germ phobias or delusions of self-importance. She is not manipulative, malicious or moody, nor inept, indecisive or idle. She actually likes the human race and doesn't want to take revenge on them for her miserable childhood. She will trust her staff and respect you as equals. She won't panic when she can't see you, and imagine you have climbed out the window and absconded down the drainpipe, when you are quietly getting on with your work. She won't loom up behind you to check whether you are updating your profile on Facebook. She won't deluge you with pointless paperwork that detracts from important work.

Genevieve has great insight into people and adapts her management style according to the job in hand – she won't use the same management style for a large civil service department as for a small team of people in a tiny office. If there are any piss-takers, Genevieve will recognize them and deal with them accordingly. She won't avoid confronting the piss-takers and get more heavy-handed with the staff who are doing their job, because it's easier than dealing with the piss-takers. She won't haul you over the coals for taking an extra three minutes on your lunch break, and then ignore the piss-taker who spends all his time on his mobile phone running a money transfer business on the side.

If you are a conscientious worker and you start having problems with your work, Genevieve will be patient and sympathetic. She will try to find out if it is a personal issue, or whether it is related to the office. She will give you the time and confidentiality to talk about it and find a solution. If you become stressed, Genevieve won't accuse you of time management problems when in fact you're suffering burnout. If you fall ill and take a couple of days off sick, she will believe you are sick, and will ask you how you feel when you return. Similarly if your child is ill or your childcare arrangements break down, Genevieve will allow you time off to sort it out.

Genevieve is confident in her own abilities. She doesn't mind admitting if she has made a cock-up and she won't blame the nearest staff member to cover her arse. She isn't threatened by talented staff because she knows that a good staff team will be an asset to the organization and reflect well on her. She likes to give people the opportunity to develop their skills and careers. You will actually look forward to coming to work with Genevieve as a manager. You will feel optimistic about your career, and you will want to give your best. You won't mind working hard and doing extra hours if necessary because you know it will be appreciated.

Oh Genevieve, elusive angel, where are you? Why will we never find you in offices across the land?

FOR DEALING WITH GENEVIEVE

If you do have a manager like Genevieve, stick with your job, because having a good manager will transform your life. Become a manager yourself and be like Genevieve. Set up a management school and train managers to be like Genevieve. Fall pregnant and start an army of managers like Genevieve. Build up your numbers, spread the word and fight to rid the world of crap managers.

31960756R00074

Printed in Great Britain
by Amazon